Praise for
Embrace Grace

"Liz Curtis Higgs is a gifted writer and poet who understands the human heart with all its complexity, beauty, and pain. She also understands the heart of God. Reading this book will make you want to let go of anything that keeps you from his loving embrace. I recommend it highly."

—REBECCA PIPPERT, best-selling author
of *Out of the Saltshaker & into the World*

"For every woman who has ever felt as if she were standing on the outside looking in, welcome home! In *Embrace Grace,* Liz Curtis Higgs gently addresses the lies that keep us from everything our hearts so desperately need: love, forgiveness, and most of all, acceptance. Don't stand out there shivering in the cold! Christ stands with open arms waiting to love you back to life."

—JOANNA WEAVER, best-selling author
of *Having a Mary Heart in a Martha World*

"*Embrace Grace* isn't for perfect, churchy women who have never made a mistake. It's for women who've blown it and are willing to investigate a better way to live. Liz Curtis Higgs is vulnerable, authentic, honest, and compassionate. *Embrace Grace* provides answers, truth, and a map that will take you from shame and guilt to a hope-filled future."

—CAROL KENT, author of *When I Lay My Isaac Down*

"Leave it to Liz Curtis Higgs—a master writer, storyteller, and Bible teacher—to give us a book with a heavy-hitting message wrapped in a cloak of warmth that melts even the coldest heart. Liz tells the story of grace, forgiveness, and restoration that every one of us—the wounded, the hurting, the seeking— needs to hear. This book must be read slowly and on bended knee, for each page is steeped with truth that will cause you to more passionately embrace the Father, embrace forgiveness, and *Embrace Grace*."

—PRISCILLA SHIRER, author of *He Speaks to Me*

"Like an expert masseuse, Liz kneads away the knots of guilt, fear, and regret we all have. *Embrace Grace* speaks life-changing truth to our hurting, anxious souls in a uniquely winsome way."

—DEE BRESTIN, best-selling author
of *The Friendships of Women*

Embrace GRACE

OTHER BOOKS BY LIZ CURTIS HIGGS

Nonfiction
Bad Girls of the Bible
Really Bad Girls of the Bible
Unveiling Mary Magdalene
Rise and Shine

Historical Fiction
Thorn in My Heart
Fair Is the Rose
Whence Came a Prince
Grace in Thine Eyes

Contemporary Fiction
Mixed Signals
Bookends

Children's Books
The Pumpkin Patch Parable
The Parable of the Lily
The Sunflower Parable
The Pine Tree Parable
Go Away, Dark Night

Embrace
GRACE

Welcome
TO THE
FORGIVEN
LIFE

LIZ CURTIS HIGGS

WATERBROOK
PRESS

EMBRACE GRACE
PUBLISHED BY WATERBROOK PRESS
12265 Oracle Boulevard, Suite 200
Colorado Springs, Colorado 80921
A division of Random House Inc.

Scripture quotations are taken from the Holy Bible, New International Version®. NIV®. Copyright © 1973, 1978, 1984 by International Bible Society. Used by permission of Zondervan Publishing House. All rights reserved.

10-Digit ISBN: 1-4000-7218-2
13-Digit ISBN: 978-1-4000-7218-7

Library of Congress Cataloguing-in-Publication Data
Higgs, Liz Curtis.
   Embrace grace : welcome to the forgiven life / Liz Curtis Higgs. — 1st ed.
      p. cm.
   ISBN 1-4000-7218-2
   1. Christian women—Religious life. 2. Forgiveness of sin. 3. Grace (Theology)
I. Title.
   BV4527.H538 2006
   248.8'43—dc22

                              2006013147

Printed in the United States of America
2006—First Edition

10 9 8 7 6 5 4 3 2 1

For my precious friend, Glenna Salsbury,
who lives grace, teaches grace,
exudes grace

And for my dear husband, Bill,
who embraced this Former Bad Girl
and never let go

CONTENTS

An Open Door 1
"I don't feel like I belong anywhere."

Embrace Doubt 19
"The whole thing seems a little hard to believe."

Embrace Faith 35
"How do I find the faith to touch him?"

Embrace Truth 49
"I always felt like I was missing something."

Embrace Sin 65
"How could he love me after all I've done?"

Embrace Forgiveness 87
"Can I know for sure that God has forgiven me?"

Embrace Repentance 113
"Striving for perfection can be exhausting."

Embrace Grace 133
"What a freeing experience!"

A Last Word from Liz 147

We have peace with God
through our Lord Jesus Christ,
through whom we have gained
access by faith
into this grace
in which we now stand.

ROMANS 5:1–2

An
Open
Door

See, I have placed
before you
an open door
that no one can shut.

REVELATION 3:8

I've been waiting for you. Holding this good news close to my heart, longing to share it.

And now here you are, standing on the threshold.

To say that I'm glad to see you is a major understatement. *Thrilled* is more like it. Curb my enthusiasm? No way. Not when it's *you*.

There are a few things about you that I don't know: your age, your appearance, your occupation. Facts that describe you but don't define you and have little bearing here.

There are also things about you that I do know because we share them: the need to be loved unconditionally, the desire to live a life that truly matters, the longing to shed a tightly woven mantle of guilt.

Or am I the only woman who wears past failures and present mistakes like an old wool coat, scratchy and uncomfortable, chafing the skin around my neck?

Ah. You too.

Sadly, heavy overcoats get in the way of a good hug. Our arms are too stiff, our bodies too padded. No one can sense our warmth through the thick fabric.

In the same way, remorse and shame insulate us. And isolate us.

If only we could toss those miserable garments into some dark closet and tiptoe away. If only the ratty things didn't feel so cozy and familiar. If only we could shake off the conviction that we *need* to wear our guilt—deserve to wear it, must wear it—whatever the season.

Maybe it's time to release that burden and lift our arms toward the One who loves us most.

That's what this visit is all about: slipping off the old and putting on the new. Letting go of the past and embracing freedom with our whole hearts.

Come inside where it's warm, beloved.

Let me help you with your coat.

Take hold of the life
that is truly life.
1 Timothy 6:19

The forgiven life. The grace-filled life.

It begins with an embrace, which is more than an elegant word for *hug*.

Hugs are short-lived and friendly, handed out like after-dinner mints to acquaintances and strangers alike.

Here, have one.

An embrace is more intentional. Longer. Warmer. Far more personal.

We gather someone close—a spouse, a child, a friend, a sibling—and murmur words of comfort and affection. Or we simply let the strength of our embrace express the depth of our thoughts and feelings.

I believe in you.

I support you.

I treasure you.

I love you.

Wherever you are spiritually, whatever you have been through emotionally, you are already wrapped in the Lord's embrace. Held close by nail-scarred hands. Enfolded in the arms of One who believes in you, supports you, treasures you, and loves you.

He is waiting for you to embrace him in return. To accept the gift he's offering you. To listen for the whispered words you've longed a lifetime to hear:

You are loved. All is forgiven.

When the kindness

and love

of God our Savior

appeared,

he saved us,

not because of

righteous things

we had done,

but because of

his mercy.

Titus 3:4–5

"Mercy." An old-fashioned word, fraught with meaning.

"Mercy!" my friend Sara says, her hand pressed to her heart. *Mercy,* God says, yet it's our hearts he touches.

> And God is able to make
> all grace abound to you.
> *2 Corinthians 9:8*

A single syllable, *grace* is God's word for *love,* expressed through divine forgiveness.

Sometimes we respond with an even shorter word. *No.*

We persuade ourselves we have good reason to shrug off the Lord's touch and refuse his gift of grace. Consider the heartfelt words of one of my readers:

> "I don't feel I am worthy
> of having God
> forgive me of my
> sins and weaknesses.
> I feel like a failure."

How poignantly she states what we often feel! Unworthy? Me too. A failure? Oh yes. We get it.

"I feel like I have let God down,
and I can't seem to find the forgiveness I seek.
Even on Sundays I don't feel
his presence or direction,
and I long for it."

We understand that longing: to sense the realness of God, to know that he is with us, no matter what we've done. For all our good days, we've stumbled through bad ones too.

"I am struggling not to lead two separate lives—
the Good Girl versus the Bad Girl."

We're with you, sis. The battle is genuine, yet the grace of God prevails.

I cherish such words from our sisters because they remind us we're not alone. You'll hear dozens of women's voices echoing throughout *Embrace Grace*. Honest women. Hurting women. Hopeful women.

I carefully omitted any identifying details—no names or initials, no locations or occupations—and included only brief comments that speak to our shared experience of yearning for freedom, yet feeling encumbered by previous mistakes and current challenges.

"Even though I belong to God,
I sometimes feel
so unworthy
because of my past."

"I still get that heavy feeling in my chest
over who I used to be."

We feel it too—that woolly overcoat sensation—making our shoulders sag in defeat. Whether our "past" refers to some crucial mistake we made a decade ago or a poor decision last week, regret can weigh us down.

"I often carry the guilt of
'if only they knew who I used to be,
they would not like me
as much as they do.'"

I cannot speak for what "they" think, but I am certain of what God thinks. He *does* know who you used to be. And he not only likes you, he loves you. Completely.

Always has.

Always will.

For the LORD is good
and his love endures forever;
his faithfulness continues
through all generations.
Psalm 100:5

Incredible, isn't it? To imagine God's love reaching across the boundaries of time, encircling us in his ceaseless embrace. Do you yearn to feel his heavenly arms around you? Holding you, comforting you, cherishing you?

"I *want* to want
a relationship with God.
I also want somebody
to tell me that they love me
and to know they mean it."

Be assured, no one—man, woman, or child—says "I love you" with more certainty than the Lord. His regard for us goes far beyond kind words and warm feelings; his is a show-and-tell love, held up for the whole world to see.

This is how
God showed his love
among us:
He sent his one and only Son
into the world
that we might
live through him.
1 John 4:9

At times living through him seems too daunting; just living is hard enough.

"I'll never be perfect,
and God is never going to
forgive me for this,
so what's the point?"

"I have no strength left,
and I don't feel like I belong
anywhere."

You belong right here, dear one.
Looking for answers. Seeking encouragement.

"I know God has forgiven me.
Most days I believe that,
but there are some days
it is so hard to imagine."

Embrace Grace is for those hard-to-imagine days when the gospel seems too good to be true.

Forgiveness free for the asking? Not just one time but again and again, every day of our lives? No matter how often we've tried to be good and failed? No matter how hard we've tried to be bad and succeeded?

Impossible.

But that's not the word Jesus used. He called such things *possible.*

With man
this is impossible,
but not with God;
all things are possible
with God.

Mark 10:27

I know, I know. You've heard that line before, tossed at you by some well-meaning soul. It sounds good—"all things are possible"—but how does that work exactly?

Can we be sure God forgives us when we stumble? Must we say or do something specific in order to be forgiven? And what does forgiveness feel like?

> "I know the Lord
> can do all things,
> but I, on the other hand,
> need a road map."

May our conversation here serve, if not as a map, then at least as a field guide, tracing a well-worn footpath from doubt to belief, pointing us away from shame and toward hope.

Not a false hope spun from well-meaning wishes but a trustworthy hope based on the reality of countless lives changed by a leap called faith into the arms of a hero called Faithful and True.

> "God has major plans in store for me.
> I just need to follow him."

Oh, does he have plans for you! Big plans. Exciting plans. Plans that will thrust your past well behind you and place your future within your grasp.

> "For I know the plans I have for you,"
> declares the LORD,
> "plans to prosper you
> and not to harm you,
> plans to give you hope
> and a future."
> *Jeremiah 29:11*

Following him is the key. Your sisters who've traveled a similar path can point you in the right direction. But only God can lead the way.

When your friends and loved ones fail you, God remains by your side, steadfast and true. Waiting for you to turn around when you're headed in the wrong direction. Waiting for you to look up each time you feel pressed down with fear, sorrow, or regret. Waiting for you to listen to what he has to say—not with trepidation but with expectation.

> God is our refuge
> and strength,
> an ever-present help
> in trouble.
> *Psalm 46:1*

"Ever-present" is the Bible's way of saying, "24/7."

God will be there for you, however dark the hour, however tenuous your faith.

> "I really love the Lord,
> I have repented
> of my sin,
> but I have big-time
> guilt.
> Do you think God
> can still use me,
> or is it too late?"

Are you still alive, my sister? Still drawing breath?

Then it's not too late to serve the Lord you love. And never too late to find the assurance and comfort you seek.

Praise be
to the God and Father
of our Lord Jesus Christ,
the Father of compassion
and the God of all comfort.
2 Corinthians 1:3

Speaking of comfort, that itchy, old coat of yours is still in the back of the closet, should you miss it. Meanwhile, I'll do my best to keep you warm as we move from the darkness of doubt to the light of grace.

Whether you never traveled this road before, got lost somewhere along the way, or are circling back to begin again, you are welcome here.

Make yourself at home, dear woman.

Prepare your minds for action…
set your hope fully
on the grace
to be given you
when Jesus Christ
is revealed.
1 Peter 1:13

Before you turn the page...

☽ When, if ever, have you been aware of God's tender embrace?

☽ What words do you wish God would whisper in your ear?

☽ *Are* all things possible with God? How can you be sure of your answer?

EMBRACE
DOUBT

Be merciful
to those
who doubt.

JUDE 1:22

> "For a girl who's been hurt
> by almost everyone in her life,
> trust was and still is a huge issue for me.
> Trust a God I cannot see? Puhleeease!"

*I*f we're honest, trust is an issue for many of us.

From the moment we're born, we're afraid: of loud noises, of cold air, of falling. While trust begins to build as the months go by, new fears surface: of dark rooms, of meeting strangers, of being alone.

We conquer those fears as we mature, but at the deepest level we never forget them. Old fears continue to color our emotional responses and produce feelings of doubt and uncertainty.

> "I lived most of my life
> scared to death that
> I wouldn't make it into heaven
> for one reason or another."

Heaven becomes an elusive promise, like a child's toy dangling over a crib: close enough to see, but never close enough to grasp. No wonder we stop reaching, stop trusting. No wonder the light of truth seems to grow dim and shadows fill our rooms.

> "This is a very dark time for me.
> I have been feeling
> abandoned of late."

For all those dark times, here's a word of hope: God meets us where we are. Even if we aren't looking in his direction, he is always looking in ours.

> From his dwelling place
> he watches all
> who live on earth—
> he who forms the hearts of all,
> who considers everything they do.
> *Psalm 33:14–15*

"He watches all." That would include you, right now, this very minute. Does that comfort you? Make you nervous?

Or perhaps you're shaking your head in disbelief.

> "I'm not much into God.
> The whole thing
> seems a little hard to believe."

An honest statement.

The notion of God's coming to earth as an infant wrapped in swaddling clothes, then willingly dying in his early thirties to atone for the sins of an ungrateful world—well, it is far-fetched. Very far.

Beyond the limits of human imagination.

Only an infinite God could design such an effective long-range plan.

> He was chosen
> before the creation of the world,
> but was revealed in these last times
> for your sake.
> *1 Peter 1:20*

Before he created the world, the Lord was preparing to sacrifice his Son. Eons ago he was thinking of you.

Yet God's eternal nature, glorious as it sounds, may make us wonder if he's real. Because we cannot see, hear, or touch him, faith may elude us.

> "I see no evidence of God.
> I grew up as an unwanted child.
> He was never there for me,
> as far as I could tell."

How her despair must grieve her Creator, who entrusted this precious child to her parents, knowing they would not love her as he does. Knowing that, although he remained by her side, her vision would one day be clouded by neglect.

Even now God is waiting for her—for all of us—to turn away from the pain and behold the One who never abandons his own, not for a single moment.

> By day the LORD
> directs his love,
> at night his song is with me—
> a prayer to the God of my life.
> *Psalm 42:8*

A heavenly Father who loves you all day long, who listens to you sing to him at night—is that too much for you to accept, too over the top?

Your skepticism, your unbelief will find shelter here. Doubt is where many of us began our spiritual journeys, even if we were raised in homes where religion held sway.

> "I grew up in a hard-core Christian family
> with no love, no respect,
> and no second chances.
> I was never good enough."

If you are nodding in empathy, then I have wonderful news: *no one* is good enough except God himself, who made us in his image and loves us as we are. We will never be good enough, and he will always be good enough. Off-the-chart amazing.

> You are forgiving and good, O Lord,
> abounding in love to all who call to you.
> *Psalm 86:5*

And "all" must surely mean—you got it—*all*. Including you, my friend.

Even if you doubt? Even if you're afraid? Yes, even then you can call upon God. You will hear his voice in return, in the deepest place inside you. Directing you. Forgiving you. Loving you.

> "Looking back I can now see
> God's wonderful hands
> guiding me back to him.
> God has given me a third chance to begin again."

Indeed, he gives us second chances, third, fourth, fifth chances—oh, far too many to count.

> Because of the LORD's great love
> we are not consumed,
> for his compassions never fail.
> They are new every morning;
> great is your faithfulness.
> *Lamentations 3:22–23*

You see, it's *God's* faithfulness—not ours—that makes the difference. He can handle our suspicions and fears, our misgivings and apprehensions. He is not dissuaded by our cynicism, our incredulity. He understands doubt.

"I've had so many bad things
happen in my life
that I've started to question God."

A legitimate response. Question away, sis. Confess your uncertainty.

Then relax in knowing that it's not your belief in God's existence that defines him. God simply *is*. He is love incarnate, and his righteousness endures forever.

Our doubt does not diminish God one iota.

No matter what we think, feel, or say, his praises are being sung throughout eternity.

Holy, holy, holy
is the Lord God Almighty,
who was, and is,
and is to come.
Revelation 4:8

And though our goodness is not enough, his holiness and mercy are more than enough. When we come to the end of ourselves, God is just getting started.

My grace
is sufficient for you,
for my power is made perfect
in weakness.
2 Corinthians 12:9

Wait. God expects us to be weak? More than that, beloved. He designed us in such a way that we cannot be complete without him. That unnamed longing—the emptiness we've tried to assuage with earthly relationships or material possessions or temporal pleasures—that's a need only he can meet.

"I was well aware that Jesus was out there
waiting for me
and that he could turn it all around for me,
but I just didn't care.
Finally I came crawling back to Christ,
begging him to forgive me
and fill that place again."

We may not know where "that place" inside us is or what it's called, but we know very well when it's empty. And who alone can fill it.

And so we know and rely
on the love God has for us.
God is love.
Whoever lives in love
lives in God,
and God in him.
1 John 4:16

Have you ever wondered why you are here, what the purpose is for your life? Simply this: you were made to love God and be loved by him.

If, like me, you've looked for love in all the wrong places, only to be disappointed, let me ease your doubts on this score: God, who created love before the beginning of time, will never let you down.

This is love:
not that we loved God,
but that he loved us
and sent his Son
as an atoning sacrifice for our sins.
1 John 4:10

True love is defined, not by our on-again, off-again manner of love, but by God's unchanging, never-ending love, demonstrated by the sacrifice of his own Son.

"How unfair of me
to expect him to love me
in the same way that I love."

You are so right.

God loves us even when we are unlovable.

Often our inability to accept God's perfect love for us is not a question of doubting God's love but of doubting our worthiness. Looking in the mirror of our lives, we become discouraged by what we see and disheartened by what we know to be true.

"I have many moments in my life
I am not proud of.
It's hard for me to believe
that God loves me."

Believe it, my sister, and do not doubt: God loves you. Not because you are good, but because you are his.

"I always thought
I was a Good Girl.
But the past couple of years
have been very hard for me,
and I realized I wasn't
as good as I thought."

Doubting ourselves is more promising than it sounds. The day we realize we're not perfect is the day we start asking, "Who is perfect? Who is good?"

Only one hand is raised—and his whole body with it. On the day of his resurrection, Jesus appeared to his doubting disciples. He did not punish them for their qualms; he simply addressed them.

Why are you troubled,
and why do doubts
rise in your minds?
Look at my hands and my feet.
It is I myself!
Touch me and see.
Luke 24:38–39

His invitation extends across the centuries. "Touch me and see."

This is a hands-on kind of Savior. He sees the lack of trust in our eyes, hears the dubious note in our voices, and feels the tremor in our fingers as we tentatively grasp the hem of his garment.

In the face of our doubt, the Lord offers a sure word of encouragement.

> Don't be afraid;
> just believe.
> *Mark 5:36*

BEFORE YOU TURN THE PAGE...

○ What doubts or fears—about God, about faith, about heaven—do you harbor in your heart?

○ Pinpoint any experiences in your life that might have triggered such uncertainty.

○ What would it take for you to put aside your doubts and fears and "just believe"?

EMBRACE
FAITH

We live by
faith,
not by
sight.

2 CORINTHIANS 5:7

*D*oes "just believing" sound too easy? Does it require too little on your part? Then you're on the right track. Faith is not an act of man; it is an act of God, drawing us to him.

"I am searching for a way
to get to Jesus
and I don't know
where to start.
How do I find the faith
to touch him?"

It begins with a single step. If you can place your foot on an escalator—not knowing how it works, only seeing others farther along the way, moving toward where you want to go—then you can do this. Truly, you can. One step is all that's needed.

"I really want to turn to God, but I'm so unsure.
Faith is hard for me."

I know, dearie; it's hard for everyone.
But faith is easy for God.

Let him do all the work. Take one brave step and stretch out your hand. Leave the burden of proof to him. He will not disappoint you. Remember his invitation?

"Touch me and see."

> "I know all the teaching—
> that we don't need to *feel* his forgiveness,
> only believe in it.
> But somehow
> I'm not buying that right now."

> "I can't change things by saying I trust
> what I don't know for sure is there."

Such uncertainty is understandable in a world in which feelings and facts are often valued above faith. Yet choosing to trust in the unknown does change one thing: it changes us. A newfound courage may stir within our hearts. A willingness to try something different, to exchange what is for what might be.

Risky? You bet. Faith is not something you fall back on; faith is something you step into. Like venturing inside a dark room in a stranger's house, convinced you'll find a light switch to the left of the door. Ah, there it is.

Now faith is being sure
of what we hope for
and certain
of what we do not see.
Hebrews 11:1

Hmm.

Those are words you don't often find in the same sentence. How can you be *sure* if all you have is *hope*? How can you be *certain* if you can't *see* something?

That's why faith isn't man-made; it's God-made.

Faith is a miracle born of love.

"It's hard for me to grasp
just how high
and wide
and deep
God's love is for me.
He doesn't love like I love.
He loves unconditionally."

That's it exactly: God loves us without limitations.

Higher, wider, and deeper than we can possibly imagine.

> How great is the love
> the Father has lavished on us,
> that we should be called
> children of God!
> And that is what we are!
> *1 John 3:1*

I first realized that God could be trusted—that he loved me, that I was his child—more than two dozen years ago.

When I walked through the doors of a church after a lost decade of sex, drugs, and rock'n'roll, I didn't trust God yet, but I trusted the friends who welcomed me. And I trusted them for one reason: they loved me.

> The only thing that counts is faith
> expressing itself through love.
> *Galatians 5:6*

My compassionate friends did not tell me, "Have faith." They showed me what faith looked like, how trusting in an unseen God worked in the real world. They did not say, "Believe in God," not at first. They began by saying, "God believes in you, Liz. He loves you."

God loves me? I was ready to hear more.

Maybe you're ready as well. Especially if you identify with this sister's honest admission:

> "I felt like there was no way
> God could love someone like me
> who had sinned so much."

By human standards, God's love for his people doesn't make sense. We tend to love only those who we think deserve our love and who offer us an equal measure of love in return.

> But God demonstrates
> his own love for us in this:
> While we were still sinners,
> Christ died for us.
> *Romans 5:8*

"While we were still sinners." That was the phrase that pierced my heart many years ago. God wasn't waiting for me to deserve his love or earn his forgiveness. He loved me enough to die for me *as is.*

I could put my faith in a God like that and love him in return. And so I did.

"The whole idea of pursuing
a relationship with God
is new to me.
I was raised to fear him,
not to love him."

A lightning-bolt God, then, thundering down from the heavens. Very scary, and a too-familiar image.

God does have the ability to destroy us, make no mistake. But he chooses to shower us with love instead. Not in a harsh torrent, like a thunderstorm, but in a gentle cascade, like cleansing rain.

The eyes of the LORD are on those who fear him,
on those whose hope is in his unfailing love.

Psalm 33:18

What does "those who fear him" mean? And why should we fear God if he loves us?

There are two kinds of fear. The sort that stops us in our tracks, turns our hands to ice, makes our hearts thump in our chests. Frightening, numbing fear. And the sort that bows our heads, drops us to our knees, and reminds us who is in charge and who is not. Reverent, awestruck fear.

The first kind of fear is why the phrase "do not be afraid" appears in the Bible dozens of times, assuring us that God is on our side.

The LORD himself
goes before you
and will be with you;
he will never leave you
nor forsake you.
Do not be afraid;
do not be discouraged.
Deuteronomy 31:8

Yet sometimes we *are* afraid, we *are* discouraged. By past fiascos. By present blunders. By I-hope-nobody-from-church-saw-me-do-that trepidations.

"I felt so worthless
and unworthy of God's love,
I just wanted to roll up in a ball and die.
Yet God stood by my side,
even though I was
too blind to see him."

Sometimes shame blinds us. Or we're just afraid to look. *Is he still there? Is he angry with me? Will he punish me?*

> "I can't count the times that I've really messed up,
> then found myself where I am now—
> frustrated at being back at this point,
> scared to ask for forgiveness."

I can't number all mine either, sis. It *is* frustrating. And embarrassing. *Here...again?*

Yet God doesn't want us to be afraid to come to him. That's not the "fear of the Lord" he expects from us.

Rather, he's looking for reverential fear, the kind that involves standing in awe of a Supreme Being more powerful than we are.

> For as high as the heavens are above the earth,
> so great is his love
> for those who fear him.
> *Psalm 103:11*

A constant awareness of his superiority keeps things in perspective and, frankly, takes the pressure off. If God is in charge, I don't have to be—and neither do you. What a relief!

So let your fear turn to wonder. And let your wonder turn to faith, as you believe in the One who saves you from yourself.

> The fear of the LORD leads to life:
> Then one rests content, untouched by trouble.
> *Proverbs 19:23*

Understand, life's challenges still come around. But with the Lord in control, *trouble* is no longer spelled with a capital *T*.

> For our light and momentary troubles
> are achieving for us an eternal glory
> that far outweighs them all.
> *2 Corinthians 4:17*

It is possible, then, to both fear and love God; in fact, it's necessary. All healthy relationships are built around respect, none more so than this one.

> "I finally opened my eyes to the Lord
> and realized that I didn't 'find' him.
> He was never lost—I was."

Brilliant woman, to see the truth so clearly. Her eyes have been opened—the eyes of her heart—giving her the ability to gaze upon that which cannot be seen by the human eye.

Though you have not seen him,
you love him;
and even though you do not see him now,
you believe in him
and are filled with an inexpressible
and glorious joy.

1 Peter 1:8

So much for the old saw "Seeing is believing."
God says, "*Not* seeing is believing."

"I am slowly realizing that God
is not out to destroy me.
I am becoming more and more convinced
that God loves me and forgives me."

Glory, girl! I can see the light of faith dawning on her face, can't you? That open expression, that "aha!" look, that trusting smile beginning to stretch across her features.

Never is a woman more beautiful than when she looks in the face of her Savior and sees his love for her shining in his eyes.

Let's move toward him now—not with fear but with faith.

Before you turn the page...

☙ What does "faith in God" mean to you?

☙ If you imagined Jesus looking at you, what might you see in his eyes?

☙ Since we cannot physically look upon the Lord's face, then where do we turn to "see" him?

EMBRACE
TRUTH

Your word, O LORD,
is eternal;
it stands firm
in the heavens.

PSALM 119:89

I gotta be honest: I love the Bible.

I love the stories and the lessons, I love the poetry and the psalms, and I love the wisdom I find waiting for me when I open God's Word.

If you want to know more about the Father, more about his Son, more about the Holy Spirit—and lots more about human nature—look no further: the Bible is the book for you.

And if your spiritual life is starting to wilt, nothing refreshes like Scripture.

> "At some point I turned my back
> on the One who loved me.
> My life had spiraled out of control.
> So I picked up my dusty Bible
> and started reading the Gospels.
> And I fell in love with Jesus."

We can fall in love with him all over again, just by opening his Word.

God knew hope alone would not sustain us.

We need something to hold in our hands and read with our eyes and study with our minds and speak with our mouths and store in our hearts. Something tangible. Something trustworthy. Something timeless.

> Faith comes from hearing the message,
> and the message is heard
> through the word of Christ.
> *Romans 10:17*

Whenever I long to get my heart in tune with God, I read the gospel of John. As a writer, I am overwhelmed by the beauty of the language. As a woman, I am undone by the beauty of the Savior.

> The Word became flesh
> and made his dwelling among us.
> We have seen his glory,
> the glory of the One and Only,
> who came from the Father,
> full of grace and truth.
> *John 1:14*

Oh, the imagery and the majesty of those words! "Full of grace and truth."

Now here's the rest of the story: I did not always cherish the Bible, seeing it as little more than a book of stringent rules I could not hope to follow. More than once I'd been pelted with verses of Scripture, thrown like stones meant to punish.

> "I'm surrounded by people
> who use God and their Bibles in the wrong way."

Ouch. There's the ugly truth of it. Difficult to hear, and even harder to confess that it might be *us* she's talking about. Forgive us, Lord, for all the times we've used your Word to condemn rather than to comfort.

My friends who first welcomed me to church did so for one purpose. Not so I could sing the hymns and choruses, not so I could pass the offering plate, not so I could stand up and sit down on cue. They wanted me to hear the Word of God.

And here's what I heard:

> Now as the church submits to Christ,
> so also wives should submit to their husbands.
>
> *Ephesians 5:24*

Submit?

No, no, no. Not this woman. No way.

I was single at the time, I was happy about it, and I didn't need a *man* telling me what to do. Not even a man who'd died on a cross and lived to talk about it.

> "My huge stumbling block
> was the control issue.
> I just couldn't let go,
> couldn't let his will be done."

Sometimes I think my readers not only read my books; they also read my diary.

Control? Oh my. That would be more than a stumbling block for me. That would be a brick wall only love could tear down.

On came the next verse:

> Husbands, love your wives,
> just as Christ loved the church
> and gave himself up for her.
> *Ephesians 5:25*

Christ "loved the church," his body of believers. *Loved.*

God knows us so well. We can refuse many things in life, but love is an irresistible force. Beckoning us. Wooing us. Making us consider old truth in a fresh light.

And Christ "gave himself up for her." Sounds to me like a complete relinquishment of control, an utter submission of will. The daily surrender he asks of us is nothing compared to the enormous sacrifice he's already made on our behalf.

Why would the Lord do such a thing? You know.

> I have loved you
> with an everlasting love;
> I have drawn you
> with loving-kindness.
> *Jeremiah 31:3*

When my friends first told me, "God loves you," they didn't simply speak the words; they showed me where I could find the truth for myself: "For God so loved the world..." Even a Bad Girl like me knew that verse by heart. Were there more words of encouragement to be found in Scripture? Chapters upon chapters of them, I soon discovered.

The more I read, the more I am convinced the Bible isn't simply a book.

It's a love letter.

> "I wish I could go back and change things.
> I wish I had let God be in control.
> Yet I know that my sins
> have been buried in the deepest sea,
> and he remembers them no more."

Another sister with control issues. We sooo get this.

"Yet," she says. "Yet I know…" What she knows, what she is certain of, are two promises found in God's Word and written on the tablet of her heart. Here they are, from two different centuries, from two different scribes, yet standing in complete agreement:

> You will…hurl all our iniquities
> into the depths of the sea.
> *Micah 7:19*

> …and will remember [our] sins no more.
> *Hebrews 8:12*

There's her "Yet I know" in writing.

Her assurance comes from a trustworthy source of wisdom, older than any volume on any library shelf. The Bible is the best-selling book the world has ever known, because the truths found within its pages have stood the test of time.

And so, longing to grow spiritually, we read Scripture, study it with friends, and gather on the Sabbath to hear the Word taught by a fellow pilgrim. Hour by hour, verse by verse, our faith is strengthened.

> "I was a Good Girl who derailed,
> but I am back, stronger than ever.
> I am slowly drinking my 'milk'
> to grow in God."

What got our thirsty sister back on track? God's Word—that delicious, nutritious "milk" on her menu.

> Like newborn babies,
> crave pure spiritual milk,
> so that by it
> you may grow up in your salvation.
> *1 Peter 2:2*

At first I felt uneasy opening a Bible.

What if I can't find what I'm looking for? What if I don't understand it? What if others know more than I do?

Is that you, sis? Not to worry. The Author is always on hand to offer assistance. Just ask him.

> Guide me
> in your truth
> and teach me.
> *Psalm 25:5*

> Give me
> understanding
> according to
> your word.
> *Psalm 119:169*

If someone in your circle of friends knows more about the Bible, urge her to teach you, one on one or with a partner. Don't be embarrassed to seek help. None of us becomes part of God's family because of *what* we know but because of *Whom* we know.

Even knowing God and knowing his Word, we can find ourselves in need of solace.

> "Though I've asked God's forgiveness
> and have repented,
> I feel like I can't go back to church
> because of what I've done.
> For the past month I have had my face
> buried in the Bible,
> and I still feel like I'm a failure."

Lift your head, precious one. Take a long, deep breath and let me dry your tears. Though you may have failed in some ways—just as I have, just as every member of your congregation has—you are not a failure, not by any means.

The Bible can provide all the encouragement you need to walk through the doors of your church. Not with your head held high with pride nor bowed low with shame. Simply make your way toward the nearest pew with his Word in your hands and his promise in your heart:

> The LORD is with me; I will not be afraid.
> What can man do to me?
>
> *Psalm 118:6*

In the end, man (or woman) can do nothing to you of eternal significance. And, as the Bible tells us, God can do everything.

> "I always felt like I was missing something
> but could not put my finger on it.
> Now I know what it was—God."

Whatever circuitous route led her to God, you can be sure his Word illumined her path.

> Send forth your light and your truth,
> let them guide me.
> *Psalm 43:3*

The couple who encouraged me to visit their church years ago also welcomed me into their home, where a well-worn Bible always lay within reach. At first I found it strange that they turned to a *book* to address my various questions about God. If they loved him so much, didn't they already know the answers?

"No," they insisted. "Better to reach for the source than bluff our way through."

I had to admit, the passages they read aloud made sense. A lot of sense, actually.

Before long, I wanted a study Bible of my own—one identical to theirs so I could look things up by *page number.* No, I'm not kidding. I knew zip about Scripture. Second Chronicles sounded the same as Second Corinthians to me. (Half the time I still have to start with Genesis and mentally run through the books of the Old Testament to find the one I'm looking for!)

Did my inexperience get in the way of God's teaching me? Not for one minute. He made me so hungry for his Word that every evening I sat at the dining room table like a ravenous woman, hovering over my new Bible, salivating over every sentence.

> I have treasured the words of his mouth
> more than my daily bread.
> *Job 23:12*

I remember the day I found one vital passage in particular. Reading it aloud to a group of friends, I was so moved that I ended up weeping. To think that *nothing* could separate us from God's love! Perhaps you are stronger than I am and can recite this without your throat tightening or your eyes watering. As for me, I'm reaching for a tissue…

> For I am convinced that neither death nor life,
> neither angels nor demons,
> neither the present nor the future,
> nor any powers, neither height nor depth,
> nor anything else in all creation,
> will be able to separate us
> from the love of God
> that is in Christ Jesus our Lord.
> *Romans 8:38–39*

Nothing. *Nothing* in all creation.

For those of us who've done *everything* in God's creation to ignore him, offend him, or deny him, these words offer incredible hope.

We're not too late. We've not gone too far. We didn't blow it completely.

God is on our side. God loves us still.

> "That verse changed everything for me.
> I sobbed so hard, my heart burst open.
> God moved in and caulked the broken places.
> He was there for me and has been there for me
> every day, every moment since."

Before you turn the page...

☼ What place does God's Word hold in your heart? in your home? in your day-to-day life?

☼ Read aloud a verse of Scripture from this chapter that has challenged you, changed you, or comforted you. Why are those words especially meaningful to you?

☼ If it's time to take the next step in your spiritual journey, how might God's Word help you move forward?

EMBRACE
SIN

If we claim to be
without sin,
we deceive ourselves
and the truth
is not in us.

1 JOHN 1:8

*O*nce honest doubt is acknowledged and genuine faith takes the lead, once the Word of God has been accepted for the truth that it is, the next step is inevitable. And unavoidable.

Because when we look upon the beauty of Christ in Scripture, we encounter our own ugliness. Compared to his sinless life, our own lives are—let's face it—a mess.

"I just wanted to be accepted…"

"All I wanted was to be loved…"

"I am so selfish…"

The truth is, we all sin. All of us. All the time. Still.

Who can say,
"I have kept my heart pure;
I am clean and without sin"?
Proverbs 20:9

Not me, babe. Not for a minute.

Even if we embraced Christ as our Savior decades ago, we still sin. We sinned before we knew he existed, and we've sinned after. We feel guilty, of course, but still we sin. And beat ourselves up unmercifully.

"I could not accept
that Christ could see past my sins—
after all, I had been a Good Girl.
I knew better!"

Bad Girls know better too, however dark our foolish hearts. We may look the other way, feign indifference, or ignore the rules, but we know what those rules are and who made them.

For since the creation of the world
God's invisible qualities—
his eternal power and divine nature—
have been clearly seen,
being understood from what has been made,
so that men are without excuse.

Romans 1:20

However loudly we may protest that God doesn't exist, the truth is all around us.

And the reality of our sin is even more undeniable.

If we take a peek in our mirrors, do we see any evidence of sin? How about our calendars—any less-than-holy activities there? Are all the thoughts running through our minds pure? Is every television program we watch spiritually edifying? Does every word that falls from our lips sweeten the air? Do our children rise up and call us blessed?

Okay, okay, I'll stop. No need to elaborate when the truth is so obvious.

> For I know my transgressions,
> and my sin is always before me.
> *Psalm 51:3*

Always. Right there.

One woman's sins may be less dramatic than another's. Your latest transgression may not make the nightly news or raise eyebrows when confessed among friends. But any sin, no matter how seemingly small, mars our souls and grieves our spirits. We still have to fess up.

> If we claim
> we have not sinned,
> we make him out to be a liar
> and his word
> has no place in our lives.
> *1 John 1:10*

The place God's Word holds in our lives is crucial. Because interspersed among the verses that uplift and inspire us are equally important verses that admonish and convict us. You know…the verses we don't underline or memorize. The ones we gloss over, hoping they mean something other than what they clearly state.

> For whoever keeps
> the whole law
> and yet stumbles
> at just one point
> is guilty of breaking
> all of it.
> *James 2:10*

One little sin or a zillion, we're still sinners who need a Savior.

Even verses that encourage us to do good can make us feel guilty, reminding us how far from the mark we fall.

The wisdom that comes from heaven
is first of all pure;
then peace-loving, considerate, submissive,
full of mercy and good fruit,
impartial and sincere.
James 3:17

On our best days, we might manage some of the above, and so we pluck out those words like ripe fruit tugged from a pear tree. *Sure I love peace. Sincere? That's me.*

But what about the other godly attributes? *Merciful. Considerate. Submissive...again.* Do we pretend those words aren't there? Leave them for other believers to claim? Insist they're not among our spiritual gifts?

Sometimes in desperation we give up trying.

"I thought I was the worst girl ever to have lived
and that it was hopeless
for someone like me to be redeemed."

"Hopeless." The saddest of words.

Sin not only separates us from God; it separates us from one another. We go underground, hiding from those who seem good and holy, convinced we are, as our honest sister admits, "the worst girl ever."

Pressed down by a painful awareness of our sins, we feel powerless to lift our heads.

> My guilt
> has overwhelmed me
> like a burden
> too heavy to bear.
> *Psalm 38:4*

Just reading that verse, I slump in my chair, feeling the weight of my sinful nature, thinking of all the big and small ways I've failed the people I love most.

> "It seems I am always looking back at things
> I should have done or could have done,
> wishing I'd done this or that
> or wishing I'd done it better."

Regret is guilt with a thirty-year mortgage. No matter how many emotional payments we make, we never reduce the principal. The stain of sin remains.

> "I was filled with such guilt,
> such a longing to be loved,
> and a feeling of being unforgivable
> and dirty before God."

How we empathize with her. We know in our hearts we should confess our sins to the Lord, yet we often run in the opposite direction. Out of fear. Out of shame.

> "I was terrified of God
> and tried to hide from him...
> but there was nowhere to hide."

Here's the breathtaking truth about God and sinners: he *delights* when we come to him, confessing our transgressions. Not so he can gloat or make us grovel, but so he can lavish us with attention, heal our wounds, and remind us that our sins were atoned for at Calvary. Because he loves us, we can go before him with fear and trembling, certain of his response.

This is the one
I esteem:
he who is humble
and contrite in spirit,
and trembles at my word.
Isaiah 66:2

He *esteems*—respects, favors, regards, values, admires—a penitent sinner? Yes, he does. Not *punishes.* Not *looks down on.* Not *ignores.*

I have not come
to call the righteous,
but sinners
to repentance.
Luke 5:32

Humbled by failure, broken in spirit, quaking in our boots, ready to confess, we are at last prepared to embrace the reality of our sin and the gift of his grace.

Listen to your sisters.

"I knew I was a sinner,
knew I deserved hell
and that I could offer Jesus nothing.
That was all he wanted to hear.
And that I was willing
to accept his death
for my salvation."

I can hear the angels rejoicing, can't you? "She's got it! That's *it*!"

"I gave up and said, 'Forget it.
I am so done with this God thing.
I will never be good enough.'
But God kept speaking to me
about getting it right with him.
He just wants a relationship.
That I can do."

That's precisely what God wants: a relationship with you. And you *can* do it. Not because you are good enough, but because he is good enough.

> "I confessed
> my sinful past
> to the Lord
> and asked for his
> forgiveness.
> Now I am healing!"

Yes, yes, a thousand times yes!

We only appreciate God's grace when we realize how desperately we need it every day of our lives. To strive to follow all the rules and refuse to admit we ever sin denies the power of the cross.

> "Sometimes I wonder,
> how could he love me after all I've done?
> Yet I know he was nailed to the cross
> and gave his life for me—*for me*!"

> "I realize that the same drop of blood
> that was shed for me
> was shed for us all.
> He loves me—he loves us all—that much."

Indeed he does.

God loves us so much that he made the path from guilt to grace very straightforward. Some three thousand years ago King David—whose own sins included adultery and murder—followed four simple steps to forgiveness that still work today:

> I acknowledged my sin to you
> and did not cover up my iniquity.
> I said, "I will confess my transgressions
> to the LORD"—
> and you forgave
> the guilt of my sin.
> *Psalm 32:5*

It's a path well worth following.

Embrace your sin.

Shine a light on it.

Confess your sin to God.

Receive his grace.

Not just the first time we realize we've sinned—every time. Why let sins stack up until we're bent over with guilt? Embrace, shine, confess, and receive. Done.

And here are the far greater steps God takes once we've done our small part.

> If we confess our sins,
> he is faithful and just
> and will forgive us our sins
> and purify us
> from all unrighteousness.
> *1 John 1:9*

Forgiveness would be gift enough, but God also purifies us—gives us a spiritual bath, scrubs our souls clean—and helps us begin anew.

Now *that's* grace.

> "You name it, I have done it,
> and through the grace
> of our awesome God,
> I am washed clean!"

And he washes us over and over. Forgiving and cleansing. Every time, for every sin.

"God doesn't go back—
he has forgiven
and forgotten my sins.
He loves me
again and again.
Unbelievable!"

Believe it, dear sister. And spread the good news. We must embrace our sin only long enough to confess it. And then oh-so-gladly leave it in the hands of the One who will put it out of sight and out of mind. Forever.

As far as the east
is from the west,
so far has he removed
our transgressions from us.
Psalm 103:12

However far you care to travel—east to South Africa or west to South Asia—you won't discover your past failures waiting for you at baggage claim.

Those old sins are gone from sight.

> "I have learned that
> God is bigger
> than any sin
> I have committed.
> I am not ashamed anymore."

Oh, to be done with shame for good!

When we confess our sins, they no longer exert any power over us. Such freedom isn't a mental illusion; it's a physical and spiritual reality.

> "I felt my chest get warm,
> like there was a hand around my heart,
> and I knew at that moment
> I was indeed loved."

You *are* loved. And there's plenty left for the rest of us. His love is limitless.

> "Not only do I know I'm forgiven,
> but I'm also aware that
> I'm not the only person who struggles.
> What a load off my shoulders!"

I hear the sound of another heavy wool coat hitting the floor, don't you?

Ahhh.

It is for freedom
that Christ has set us free.
Galatians 5:1

No question, when you confess your sins to God, it's a liberating step forward.

Now I wonder if you might consider taking an even braver step by confessing your sins to another person? Maybe even (gulp) lots of persons? Among a small, safe circle of friends, perhaps. Even sharing the truth with one trusted sister can help us truly embrace, then release, our sins for good.

"Most Christians I know
don't have a 'before,'
and so I find myself
holding my story
close to my heart."

A form of self-protection we all understand.

Yet here's what I've learned after two dozen years of embracing the forgiven life and speaking openly about my Former Bad Girl self: many Christians *do* have a "before" and are waiting anxiously for others to confess their stories so they can too.

> "I wish people at church
> could just be real
> and stop pretending."

> "I feel like a Bad Girl
> who has never had a chance
> to tell anyone
> just how bad I've been,
> thus making it harder to heal
> and to feel more accepted
> by other Christians."

Our sisters are on to something: acceptance and healing can be found in admitting the truth about our weaknesses. Being real with one another. No longer pretending to be Good Girls when we know in our hearts we are sinners, wholly dependent on the grace of God.

> Therefore confess your sins to each other
> and pray for each other
> so that you may be healed.
> *James 5:16*

I realize what I'm asking of you. Better still, what God may be asking of you.

When considering when and where to air our sins, we need to weigh the consequences, including the possibility of hurting those we love. Only you and the Lord know if a public confession—a testimony, if you will—might serve the greater good.

You have every right to be nervous about the idea. The first time I shared my I-once-was-lost-but-now-am-found story, I stood in front of five hundred friends and strangers, having never given a speech of any length, let alone to so large a crowd, let alone on so personal a subject.

I was petrified.

My only consolation was knowing my story might offer a suffering sister hope, showing her how to expose her wounds to the light of God's love and be healed, just as I was. Just as many have been.

And you never know who might be listening.

When Jesus healed a bleeding woman, he looked around to see who had touched his garment. Though she shook with fear, she moved forward—so brave, this unnamed woman!—and made her confession before a crowd of strangers.

Then the woman,
knowing what had happened to her,
came and fell at his feet and, trembling with fear,
told him the whole truth.
Mark 5:33

"The whole truth." Holding nothing back. Now that's being real. We know the rest of that happy story. Her faith—and his grace—released her from her suffering.

So if the Son sets you free,
you will be free indeed.
John 8:36

Freedom: it's what all of us yearn for.

"I have struggled with guilt,
and it has held me back long enough."

Yes, it has, beloved. Embrace your sin, but don't hold on to it. Forgiveness is a much better fit.

Before you turn the page...

○ How—and how often—do you confess your sins? Do you pray about them? Write them out in your journal? Share them with a trusted friend?

○ Are there secret sins in your life that *no* one knows about? Might you be willing now to whisper them, knowing that only the Lord is listening?

○ An old Scottish proverb states, "Open confession is good for the soul." How might going public with our past help our hearers? And how might it benefit us?

EMBRACE
FORGIVENESS

I write to you,
dear children,
because your sins
have been forgiven
on account of his name.

1 JOHN 2:12

"I don't think I've been able
to forgive myself
because part of me doesn't believe
that I deserve to be forgiven."

*H*ow I wish this were an isolated comment, lifted from a single, heartbreaking e-mail. But I've heard the same confession from hundreds of women all over the world.

"I still feel after all my praying
that I deserve to go to hell for what I've done."

"I haven't reached the point
where I can talk about my past.
The shame lingers.
Can I know for sure
that God has forgiven me,
even if I can't forgive myself?"

Oh, my sister. If forgiveness were offered only to those who deserve it, we would all be doomed. Every one of us.

Here's one verse we often use as a hickory switch, thrashing ourselves whenever we stumble:

> All have sinned
> and fall short of the glory of God,
> *Romans 3:23*

And that's true, of course. We *have* sinned. We've already embraced that reality. We know we fall short of perfection. Way short.

But notice something interesting about that familiar verse: it ends in a comma. Meaning sin is not the whole story. Check out the rest of the sentence:

> and are justified freely
> by his grace
> through the redemption
> that came by Christ Jesus.
> *Romans 3:24*

We're not to stop at sin, then; we're to move on to grace. Freely. No payment on our part is required, because the cost has already been paid in full, and we've been redeemed.

To redeem a gift certificate, you hand over a piece of paper—purchased by someone else and inscribed with your name—in exchange for something of value yet at no cost to you.

You've done nothing to deserve this free gift. You simply hold out your hands and say, "Thank you."

That's grace in a nutshell. A gift. A *gift*. With a tag that reads, "For you."

Here's another verse we chop in half and use as a whip:

> For the wages of sin
> is death,
> *Romans 6:23*

Our shoulders sag as we nod in agreement. *That's me. I've sinned. Now I have to pay for it.* Do you really? Read the rest of the verse:

> but the gift of God
> is eternal life
> in Christ Jesus
> our Lord.
> *Romans 6:23*

How often we've fixated on the first part of that truth and ignored the second. We hear "sin" and "death" and completely miss "gift of God" and "eternal life."

No wonder we find it so hard to forgive ourselves.

We're thinking *punishment.*

God is thinking *Christmas.*

> Thanks be to God
> for his
> indescribable gift!
> *2 Corinthians 9:15*

What was the best present you ever found waiting beneath the Christmas tree? The one you didn't ask for because you didn't know such a glorious thing existed? Mine was a lovely spinning toy, shaped like a colorful tulip, which unfolded to reveal a dancing ballerina.

Oh, was it something!

And it *is* indescribable, because my words aren't doing it justice, and I can't think of what to call it. But I know it was real. I still have a faded color photo of me on my fifth Christmas, cradling that mysterious gift with a look of wonder on my face.

That's the kind of gift God has for you. Wonderful. Indescribable. Yet gloriously real. *Grace.*

I feel you tugging at my sleeve, whispering in my ear. "Liz, I know all this in my head. But my heart refuses to believe it."

I hear you. Grace is unbelievable. Beyond comprehension. Miraculous. That's why it's a gift only the Creator of the universe could give.

> "I am praying that women
> will feel safe enough
> to accept the gift of grace.
> For many,
> the wounds run so deep
> that the gift is a mystery."

It *is* hard to receive a gift you feel you don't deserve. More than once I've blushed and stammered when someone handed me a present, usually because I didn't feel worthy of such generosity or because I didn't have something to give in return.

But forgiveness isn't that kind of gift. It flows in one direction: from God to you. And you are worthy—not because you think so, but because he deems you so.

Let's say *you* held a priceless gift, beautifully wrapped, ready to be presented to anyone of your choosing.

Would you rather give this gift to someone who really needs it, is desperate for it, and will weep with joy when she opens it? Or someone who has no need of your gift, no interest in it, and will only glance at the contents before tossing it aside?

An easy question, with an even easier answer.

And who is the ultimate gift giver?

You're way ahead of me.

> Every good and perfect gift is from above,
> coming down from the Father
> of the heavenly lights.
> *James 1:17*

Your heavenly Father is holding out the gift of grace, purchased by his Son's blood.

No gift has ever cost more.

However large your bank account, you cannot possibly pay for it. You can only accept it, without putting any conditions on yourself or on the gift. Never mind earning it, deserving it, or working for it. You *need* it, period. You can't live without it.

I am not suggesting this is easily done. For some of us, receiving a gift can be very difficult indeed.

> "I've asked God into my life,
> yet I hold on to the pain.
> I know God loves me and wants to help me,
> but it is hard letting down
> that wall I've put up."

How wise you are, my sister, to be aware that *you* put up that wall. No doubt to protect yourself from getting hurt. To keep away intruders who are not looking out for your best interests.

Some of our walls were built during childhood to hold an abusive parent at bay. Others were constructed through our teen years to shut out the cruel taunts of our classmates. Bricks may have been added when boyfriends or husbands endangered our sense of well-being.

I would never ask you to dismantle walls that make you feel safe. Only God can do that. And he will, gladly, when you are ready. In the meantime, I wonder if you might think about installing a door. Thick and sturdy enough to protect you, yet able to swing open at his quiet knock.

"I am a fallen Christian
who made the mistake of trying to gain grace
rather than allowing it to come into my life."

An honest and very human mistake. Many of us have tried building a ladder to heaven rather than opening the doors of our hearts. A ladder demonstrates the work we've undertaken to earn our way upward, rung by rung, nail by nail. "See?" we say proudly, holding up our handiwork.

But a certain carpenter named Jesus already stretched his arms over a length of wood and was nailed there for your benefit. We cannot add to his work, dear one. When he said, "It is finished" (John 19:30), he meant it.

Yet we can do something: we can fully embrace God's forgiveness and allow him inside our hearts and lives. Even when we're hurting and don't care to talk, he wants to be with us. You don't have to cook anything, make your house presentable, or try to act cheerful. Just open the door and let him in.

So do not fear, for I am with you;
do not be dismayed, for I am your God.

Isaiah 41:10

Still, many of us *are* afraid. And dismayed. Even the Good Girls among us are appalled by the depths of our sinful attitudes, by our hidden (and not-so-hidden) transgressions—anger, pride, jealousy, cruelty—knowing we're called to be patient, humble, generous, and kind.

> "I have never doubted God existed,
> but I have always struggled with my BadGirlness
> and with the concept and practice of being
> a 'good' or 'strong' Christian."

Right. And so we read that promise from God in Isaiah—"I am with you"—and the words touch us deeply, yet we remain unwilling to change.

We go to church, we hang out with other Christians, and then when no one is looking, we do what we please, rather than what pleases God.

We feel powerless to explain why. And even more powerless to stop sinning.

Forgive ourselves? Not this year, not likely.

> "I love God and don't understand
> why I walk according to the flesh.
> I have so much shame."

Lowered chins. Averted eyes. Heated cheeks. We know what shame looks and feels like. We've been there. Some days we're still there.

> "I don't know how
> to stop being bad.
> I know Jesus loves me,
> but I slip into old behavior patterns."

We feel stuck. Like we can't move, can't breathe, and definitely can't change. It's not true, but it sure feels true.

> "I can't be good. I *can't.*
> I'm feeling really alone right now
> and kind of scared."

> "I live a parallel life and I'm miserable.
> I fear no one will love me
> or trust me again.
> I am certain I cannot do this alone."

How very right you are. None of us can manage this solo.

Not even Paul, the greatest of the apostles. Listen to the cry of his heart:

I do not understand
what I do.
For what I want to do
I do not do,
but what I hate
I do.
Romans 7:15

Doesn't that sum up the whole problem for those of us who've confessed Christ yet still struggle with sin? Doing what we shouldn't do. Not doing what we should do. Shoulda-woulda-coulda circa AD 57.

For another eight verses, Paul wrestles with two fierce opponents raging inside him: heavenly longing versus human desire. He concludes with an anguish we all share:

What a wretched man I am!
Who will rescue me
from this body of death?
Romans 7:24

Then the answer comes. And it isn't Paul rescuing himself; it's God rescuing Paul.

Thanks be to God—
through Jesus Christ our Lord!

Romans 7:25

No, I didn't leave anything out between Paul's cry of pain and his exclamation of joy. Nothing comes between "Help!" and "Hallelujah!"

Paul knew he could add nothing to the gift. Nor did he have to wait until God was in the mood to be generous.

With God, it's always Christmas.

And always Easter.

The gift of his Son's birth.

The gift of his Son's blood.

The greatest of gifts, meant for you. Meant for us all.

How much more did God's grace
and the gift that came by the grace
of the one man, Jesus Christ,
overflow to the many!

Romans 5:15

Here's another unexpected gift: the concept of "forgiving yourself" doesn't appear in the Bible. Surprised? Me too, because it certainly appears in my mailbox. Often.

> "Since I've never been able
> to forgive myself,
> I thought,
> 'Why would God forgive me either?'"

> "I don't know how to approach
> that very last step of self-forgiveness."

It sounds reasonable, this need to forgive ourselves. A natural, human desire. Yet it's the absolute *opposite* of grace, which is supernatural and beyond human ability.

God's forgiveness is all we need. His grace is enough. Truly *enough*.

> "I felt unforgivable,
> but that's underestimating God."

You are so right, sis. God isn't simply a larger version of ourselves. He is *God*. Maker of the heavens and the earth and us.

To say that you're willing to accept God's forgiveness but cannot forgive yourself is to say you value your opinion above God's.

Shaky ground, that.

> Who is like
> the LORD our God,
> the One who sits
> enthroned on high?
> *Psalm 113:5*

No one is like our sovereign Lord. If he says you are forgiven—and he does—then you are. You cannot add or subtract from his gift of grace.

> "It has taken over twenty years
> for me to understand
> that God has forgiven me."

He forgave you long ago, dear woman. No need to spend two decades—or two years or two months or even two days—seeking forgiveness. God's mercy was extended to you two *thousand* years ago. In truth, farther back than that.

This grace was given us in Christ Jesus
before the beginning of time.
2 Timothy 1:9

Before time was set in motion, forgiveness was waiting
for you.

Mind-boggling.

And with two words his forgiveness is yours: "I believe."

For it is with your heart
that you believe
and are justified,
and it is with your mouth
that you confess
and are saved.
Romans 10:10

God has made forgiveness so simple that even a child can
respond.

If anyone acknowledges
that Jesus is the Son of God,
God lives in him and he in God.
1 John 4:15

We adults, however, try to complicate things, refusing to believe that anything worth having can be obtained without substantial human effort.

> "I've wrestled with
> allowing God to forgive me
> for something
> I was unable to forgive myself for.
> Finally I realized
> I had to let go.
> It was as if
> a weight was lifted."

Yet another woolly overcoat bites the dust. Don't you love it? Shame and regret are gone. For good.

> "I am a ton lighter emotionally
> and am finally back on track."

We can hear the certainty in her words and feel the spring in her step. She didn't have to forgive herself; she simply had to accept God's forgiveness, knowing his grace is all she needs.

"I am a Christian who backslid, faltered,
whatever you want to call it."

We understand, sis. It's just called *sin.* A common affliction.

"I could not forgive myself,
even after I realized that
our beautiful and merciful God
truly and completely forgave me."

Her deep regard for the Lord is apparent; so is her self-reproach.

Thank the Lord, he loves us too much to let us drown in our sorrow. And so he tenderly opens our hearts so the guilt can pour out.

"Then I was completely broken.
We're talking
true repentance here."

Oh yes, we're with you. Completely broken, completely forgiven. It truly *is* finished. And notice she didn't break herself; she was broken. It's still God's work.

"After years of beating myself up,
I've gone through a sort of
death and burial of my former self
and a resurrection of my new self."

There you go, girlfriend. He went first so we might follow his example. Birth to death to new life.

Therefore, if anyone is in Christ, he is a new creation;
the old has gone, the new has come!
2 Corinthians 5:17

I love the exclamation point. *Yes!* it says. *You bet!*

That was the very first verse of Scripture I memorized, though in a different translation. Mine had the word *behold* in it. As in, *Voilà! Look at this! See for yourself!*

"I was a Bad Girl for a long time,
but through God's grace
I found my way out of that lifestyle.
Those tags and labels don't have to last forever."

No, they don't. In fact, why not delete those old descriptions from your emotional résumé?

Though I often refer to myself as a Former Bad Girl, that's only to remind me of God's grace on a daily basis. And to assure other Bad Girls that "Former" can be added to their titles too.

Every day, all around the world, women are embracing God's forgiveness and experiencing his freedom.

"God broke the chains
that held me captive.
He forgave me of all my sins.
He mended my heart."

"Those secret sins are no longer deep secrets,
and more important,
they no longer have the power to hurt me."

"Jesus has bestowed an amount of grace
on me that I cannot measure."

I know what you're thinking: "That's fine for them, Liz, but you don't know what I've done." So true.

Yet the Lord is fully aware. He's seen all of it. And he declares you *forgiven.*

The LORD searches every heart
and understands every motive
behind the thoughts.

1 Chronicles 28:9

He not only knows what you did, but he knows why you did it. He understands.

And he knows because *he was there when it happened.*

He saw all of it. Heard every vulgar word, saw every sinful deed, and discerned every ugly thought.

I'm not trying to add to your condemnation, dear sister. I'm pointing you to the only One who can take it away.

This then is how we know
that we belong to the truth,
and how we set our hearts at rest
in his presence
whenever our hearts
condemn us.
For God is greater than our hearts,
and he knows everything.

1 John 3:19–20

No matter what we've done, we can relax in his presence. Think of it! No need to tremble or hide or cower in shame. He knows everything about us and genuinely loves us—not in spite of, but *because of* who we are.

> "I now realize that guilt over my past
> comes from Satan—not God."

What a profound realization. The idea of needing to forgive ourselves comes from the accuser of the brethren, not from the Lord.

In an effort to rob grace of its power, the prince of darkness stays busy trying to convince us that God's forgiveness is conditional. That *we* have to do something. That *we* have to go first. That if *we* don't feel forgiven, it's *our* fault. He is not called "the father of lies" (John 8:44) without reason.

Guilt is an unwanted gift from below.

Grace is a much-needed gift from above.

> For he has rescued us from the dominion of darkness
> and brought us into the kingdom
> of the Son he loves, in whom we have redemption,
> the forgiveness of sins.
> *Colossians 1:13–14*

Duly rescued, we can embrace forgiveness with joyous abandon.

"I felt that all I could ever hope for were
the crumbs that fell from our Master's table.
Now I realize that,
because of what Jesus did on the cross,
I can eat and have my fill
of the Bread of Life."

There's a woman who grasps the big picture on grace. We can hear the gratitude in her voice, imagine the peace on her features, see the hope shining in her eyes—all because she's looking in the right direction. And reaching not for crumbs but for bread.

I am the living bread
that came down from heaven.
If anyone eats of this bread,
he will live forever.
John 6:51

He gave his life so we could truly live.
Thanks be to God. And God alone.

Before you turn the page...

♻ What was your best Christmas present ever, and why was it so special? What makes the gift of grace even more precious to you?

♻ Are you a wall builder, hoping to protect yourself? Or a ladder builder, trying to climb your way to heaven? What obstacles, if any, stand between you and the Lord?

♻ In what area of your life is it time to let go of the adversary's lies and receive God's complete forgiveness?

EMBRACE
REPENTANCE

The time has come....
Repent
and believe
the good news!

MARK 1:15

*A*t least once on every out-of-town trip, I drive down the wrong road by mistake. After a few miles I realize the signposts no longer match my directions. Or the map clearly shows I'm headed away from my destination, not toward it.

Arrgh. I can keep driving the wrong way, stubbornly insisting I'll get there somehow. Or I can backtrack—whining the whole time—until I reach the spot where I made a wrong turn and make the right one. At that point I am so relieved, so happy to be going in the correct direction, the whining ends and rejoicing begins.

When we come to our senses, when we see our mistakes—our failures, our sins, our spiritual bloopers—for what they are, it's time not only to confess but also to turn around and go back to where we know in our hearts we need to be.

We will not drive this road alone.

> "I turned my back on the Lord.
> I am so glad that the Lord didn't
> turn his back on me."

God will never turn his back on you, dear one. Patiently, lovingly, the Lord waits for each one of us to stop and face him once more.

He will not say, "I told you so," but rather, "I love you so."

> He is patient with you,
>
> not wanting
>
> anyone to perish,
>
> but everyone
>
> to come to repentance.
>
> *2 Peter 3:9*

"Everyone." I guess that means, well, every one of us. No matter what we've done. No matter how deliberately.

> "I always wanted to be a Bad Girl
>
> and thought it was okay
>
> to turn my back on God—
>
> he loved me anyway, right?
>
> Now my heart
>
> has changed so much."

That's what it takes: a change of heart. And then a shift in direction.

> "He has given me
> the inner strength,
> through his grace,
> to change."

If we're sorry yet keep on sinning, we're driving farther down the road that gets us no place we truly want to go.

To repent means to quit sinning, turn around, and walk back into God's embrace…

> realizing that God's kindness
> leads you toward repentance.
> *Romans 2:4*

Here's the thing: this is a well-traveled road. You are, no doubt, going to stumble along this route again someday, repenting afresh.

Rest assured, God's patience will outlast your obstinacy. He will still be there for you.

"I had a revelation:
I don't have to be perfect.
If I make a mistake,
all I have to do is
ask for forgiveness
and change my ways."

"I realized I don't have to be perfect
for him to still be working in my life!"

Hear the refrain in their comments? "I don't have to be perfect." This is a huge truth, sister. The best news in town.

"Striving for perfection
can be exhausting,
especially when you keep
failing at it!"

Honey, I know that's right.

I'm not sure which one wears me out more—the striving or the failing.

Perfectionism is all about me-me-me getting it right, then being proud of myself for doing so (and judging others who aren't perfect). Groan.

> "I have been trying to live up to all these
> 'perfect' Christian women in my church
> and I have failed every day, every hour,
> and every minute.
> I remind myself that I am not trying to
> impress these 'perfect' women;
> I am trying to walk as close to God as possible."

Amen, sis. And aren't you wise to put "perfect" in quotation marks? Because the truth is, no one is perfect, not even those who appear unblemished. Jesus himself said:

> No one is good—
> except God alone.
> *Mark 10:18*

One dear woman shared with me her journey from Good Girl to God's girl. Her sincerity—and her humility—take my breath away…

> "I was so absorbed in being religious
> and imposing those restrictions
> on everyone around me
> that I made myself deaf
> to the prodding of the Holy Spirit.
> I was *fine*.
> It was everyone else
> that needed to get their acts together
> and become as 'godly' as I was."

Girlfriend, do we get this! Either because we've behaved this way ourselves (my hand is raised) or because we've felt the sting of some "godly" person's reproof (been there too).

Yet look what happened when the Lord got her attention:

> "Then in a time of prayer
> I became overwhelmed
> with my own sinfulness.
> I was swallowed up
> with the sense of futility
> in everything I had 'done for God.'"

Oh, Lord Jesus. Why do her words touch me so? Am I there too? Doing, doing, doing for you?

> "An enormous bolt of lightning
> ripped through my delusions
> and exposed me
> for the fraud that I was.
> But it also exposed
> the power of the cross!
> Weeping, I threw myself
> at the grace of a Lord
> I had claimed
> but never known."

And I am weeping right along with her. What courage it took for this "perfect" woman to take off her mask and confess her need for grace—a need we all share.

Now she's been set free to worship a perfect God, who gets it right every time, because he is the very definition of rightness.

> He is the Rock, his works are perfect,
> and all his ways are just.
>
> *Deuteronomy 32:4*

Our perfect God not only points us in the right direction, time after time, but also walks beside us to make sure we get where we need to go.

It is God
who arms me with strength
and makes my way
perfect.
2 Samuel 22:33

And when you repent, when you humbly turn away from sin, you will have what most people claim is the one thing in life they truly desire: peace.

"There is a peace in my soul
that I longed for
but never could find
until I came to Jesus."

Our Prince of Peace. The very name helps us relax, knowing he reigns over peace, even as his peace reigns over us. For those of us with control issues, letting a peacemaker be in charge makes life a lot easier.

You will keep
in perfect peace
him whose mind
is steadfast,
because he trusts in you.
Isaiah 26:3

Repentance is all about trust.

Trusting God to be there when we turn back. Trusting him to keep his arms around us, even when we wriggle like impatient toddlers, trying to escape from his gentle yet firm embrace.

"I finally got
that whole Jesus concept.
I realized that to be a Christian
I didn't have to be a hypocrite.
I just had to be
as obedient as I could be
to show my gratitude and love
for a Savior
who would not let me go."

Her astute comments remind me of an old hymn by the Scottish preacher George Matheson, who once admitted these lyrics were the quickest bit of work he'd ever done: five minutes from first line to last, and not a word changed once it hit the page.

> O Love that wilt not let me go,
> I rest my weary soul in thee;
> I give thee back the life I owe,
> That in thine ocean depths its flow
> May richer, fuller be.

There it is, in the first line of the hymn: God loves you too much to let go.

He knows what is best for you, and that's all he wants for you.

His best. For your good.

> I will give them
> singleness of heart and action,
> so that they will always fear me
> for their own good.
> *Jeremiah 32:39*

Repentance is the hardest, bravest, wisest thing a person can do. No wonder John the Baptist went around shouting, "Repent!" He knew it would not be easy nor happen automatically. And look who responded.

> For John came to you to show you
> the way of righteousness,
> and you did not believe him,
> but the tax collectors
> and the prostitutes did.
> *Matthew 21:32*

Those Bad Boys and Bad Girls of the first century saw their need for repentance and turned toward God. Two thousand years later we can do the same.

> "With God's grace
> I am determined to overcome
> and conquer my past
> once and for all."

That determination is born of a repentant spirit. "Once and for all." You go, sis.

> "I still have a ways to go,
> but I know that I will get there—
> not in my strength,
> but in the strength of our Savior."

Her powerful declaration makes her reliance on the Lord's strength abundantly clear. It's not about getting your act together. It's about getting together with God.

> "I'm so totally not there yet,
> but thank God
> I'm not where I was."

> "I'm not out of my circumstances yet,
> but I know I will get there
> with God on my case!"

These women are turning back and moving forward with the Lord. They already know what many of us are discovering: the only way we can hope to live in peace is to live in grace. To lean completely on the Lord and on his assurance that our sins are fully paid for—past, present, and future.

Utterly forgiven, we can focus on him, instead of ourselves, and go wherever he leads.

For the grace of God that brings salvation
has appeared to all men.
It teaches us to say "No"
to ungodliness and worldly passions,
and to live self-controlled, upright
and godly lives in this present age.

Titus 2:11–12

Wait a minute, Liz. Are we back to "being good"? No, the goodness is still all God's.

Yet he is teaching us to choose wisely *for our own good.* Not to earn his favor—by his boundless mercy, we already have that—but to honor his name and demonstrate that his grace is real.

"I will never go back to that old way of living.
It was death to my spirit."

"I've been given a new life, a new nature,
and a second chance."

"I am a different person,
transformed in mind as well as body."

Transformation: that's exactly what God intends for us. How he must rejoice when we cast aside our old lives and exchange our bad attitudes for good attitudes.

Make that God attitudes.

> Put off your old self…
> be made new
> in the attitude of your minds;…
> put on the new self,
> created to be like God
> in true righteousness and holiness.
> *Ephesians 4:22–24*

Look how far down the road we've come, beloved. From admitting doubt to embracing faith, from acknowledging God's truth to facing our own sin and receiving his forgiveness.

Now comes this important step of repentance. Turning away from sin and turning toward righteousness. Being willing to change and be changed. Letting go of our feeble attempts at controlling our destinies. And realizing that God will do all the work.

> For I am the LORD, your God,
>
> who takes hold of your right hand
>
> and says to you,
>
> Do not fear; I will help you.
>
> *Isaiah 41:13*

How personal that promise is. Not "I will give you a map," but "I will take your hand."

We began this chapter talking about driving in the wrong direction and being forced to backtrack. One solution is to stop and ask a stranger for directions, though most of the time I get a lot of pointing and head scratching, leaving me more lost than ever.

God, on the other hand, goes the extra mile—literally— not only climbing into my heart but also sliding behind the wheel. *Relax. Let me drive.*

> "Jesus is leading me down a path
>
> to my true self.
>
> I no longer have to measure my worth
>
> through a man's eyes."

Nor do you need to measure your worth through a friend's eyes. Nor a parent's eyes. Nor a teacher's eyes. Only God's viewpoint counts. Only his opinion matters.

> "I am trying to recover
> from what the world thinks of me
> and focus on what God thinks of me."

A good plan for all of us.

The world—even our family, friends, co-workers, neighbors, acquaintances—will invariably disappoint us. They are working with the human model of conditional love and limited forgiveness.

God, however, is working from the divine model of unconditional love and unlimited forgiveness.

> "Although most people
> have not forgiven me,
> God certainly has."

Yes, he has.

We have only to look at the cross to know that is so.

BEFORE YOU TURN THE PAGE...

○ Has the Lord revealed to you an aspect of your life
that might require a change of heart or a shift in
direction? If so, how will you respond?

○ If you struggle with the need to be perfect, what makes
it difficult for you to accept God's grace—and your
imperfection?

○ What would true peace look like in your life?

EMBRACE
GRACE

Let us then approach
the throne of grace
with confidence,
so that we may receive mercy
and find grace
to help us in our time of need.

HEBREWS 4:16

"I've known in my head that God has
forgiven all the stuff I went through.
However, I still got that
nagging feeling that I was
'different' from other women I knew in church.
Then I gave my past completely to Christ.
What a freeing experience!"

A woman who embraces grace with both arms, who stops
fretting over her sins and begins focusing on her Savior,
who dries her tears so she can see others who are hurting—oh,
this is some kind of woman. The kind who can turn the world
right side up.

"It is so wonderful to know that God can use us
wherever we are, if we will allow him."

No small truth, that. "God can use us wherever we are."
Brand-new believer, teenage dynamo, thirty-something mama,
recommitted midlifer, silver-haired saint. Whoever, wherever,
God has plans for you.

Each one should use whatever gift he has received
to serve others,
faithfully administering God's grace
in its various forms.
1 Peter 4:10

The only time a grace-filled woman feels completely at peace is when she's being used by God for his glory. When we keep pouring his Word into our hearts—reading it on our own, hearing it taught, studying it with friends—that truth will begin spilling out. Thirsty people will sidle up to us, holding out their cups.

Whoever is thirsty,
let him come;
and whoever wishes, let him take
the free gift of the water of life.
Revelation 22:17

If folks on the sidelines feel obligated to point out our lack of qualifications—we don't know enough, aren't perfect enough, or haven't been believers long enough—we can gently remind them that God has his own agenda and his own timetable.

"I always thought I was somehow
less of a Christian
because I came to know the Lord later in life
and have a past.
Now I know that God can use
even late bloomers
to further his kingdom and help others."

Bloom on, babe. Whatever experiences reside in our past or present, God can use them to mold a brighter future for others. And rest assured, there's no such thing as a less-than Christian.

No, in all these things
we are more than conquerors
through him who loved us.
Romans 8:37

You see? Not *less than* but *more than*, because of God's love.

"I have felt inferior
to the other women in my church.
Even though God had healed me,
I still felt like I was soiled
or a second-class Christian."

Ah, but wait. Being a Christian isn't like traveling coach or first class. Imagine instead an airplane with seats that are all the same size and available to any passenger. We're either on the plane or we're not. We can rest in knowing that God purchased our tickets before the plane was built, charted the flight plan to our final destination, *and* is sitting in the pilot's seat!

A silly analogy, I know. But you get the idea: there are no second-class seats in the kingdom of God. And your grand-parents didn't have to take an earlier flight; you can be the first in your family to fly.

> "I always felt that I could never be
> a 'real Christian'
> because I don't have
> an amazing Christian heritage.
> It's taken me a long time to realize that
> God loves me
> just as much as he does someone
> who was 'born in church'!"

Amen and then some.

Real freedom comes when you discover that your own weaknesses are your strongest areas of ministry. God never wastes anything, especially not pain.

"Instead of my past being a stranglehold,
it now serves as a springboard
to tell of the great things
our God has done for me."

Has his grace grabbed you yet? Are you sensing the liberty
that a forever kind of forgiveness provides?

"I want to jump for joy
and share the good news of his love
at every opportunity!"

"I feel such joy, so loved and accepted!"

"I am truly free!
He loves me
and desires to use me,
warts and all!"

Truly free, truly loved. Exultant joy.

And those aren't warts, beloved. Just a little scar tissue from
wounds that God has healed. Such reminders give us tangible
evidence when we share our faith with others, helping them
move beyond doubt as we say with our Lord, "Touch me and
see."

> "Though at times I feel
> I'm not worthy to serve him,
> the Lord is using me."

No need to revisit that worthiness question, sis. God is indeed using you—further proof of your value to him. Besides, the Lord loves to use the least likely among us. Human wisdom often leans toward the educated, the trained, the look-good-on-paper candidates.

> But God chose the foolish things of the world
> to shame the wise;
> God chose the weak things of the world
> to shame the strong.
> *1 Corinthians 1:27*

The key phrase in that verse is "God chose." God didn't settle for less when he selected us, however foolishly we've behaved, however weak we consider ourselves to be.

God chose.

> "We are precious to God, we are his instruments,
> and he can and will use us for his glory
> despite any of our failings, doubts, or sins."

"He can and will use us." That level of confidence comes only from grace. From the blessed assurance that the blood of Christ is enough.

Enough for you. Enough for everyone you love. Enough for the whole planet.

> All over the world this gospel
> is bearing fruit and growing,
> just as it has been doing among you
> since the day you heard it
> and understood God's grace
> in all its truth.
> *Colossians 1:6*

And that truth is simple. Resist the urge to complicate it. Keep the image of a gift firmly in mind. A present you can give to others. Freely. Gladly.

> For it is by grace
> you have been saved, through faith—
> and this not from yourselves,
> it is the gift of God—
> not by works, so that no one can boast.
> *Ephesians 2:8–9*

Okay, you can boast about one thing:

> Let him who boasts boast in the Lord.
> *1 Corinthians 1:31*

David sings that truth in the Old Testament (Psalm 34:2; 44:8), then Paul brings it up twice in the New Testament. Must be important. By all means, brag on God. Give him credit for everything.

And when you're tempted to say, "Look what I did," consider adopting Paul's perspective:

> If I must boast,
> I will boast of the things
> that show my weakness.
> *2 Corinthians 11:30*

Won't *that* get people's attention! "Here's where I'm weak." Such transparency is the mark of a confident Christian. Especially when your next sentence declares, "And here's where God is strong."

"Even though I may have done things
that I'm not proud of,
God can turn it around
and use my experiences
to show his love and forgiveness
to those around me."

What humility, dear sister. How God must delight in you!
Not only do you share his love, you also show his love.
Not only do you tell others about his forgiveness; you, too,
forgive them.

Bear with each other
and forgive whatever grievances
you may have against one another.
Forgive as the Lord forgave you.
Colossians 3:13

This is the final step of our journey from doubt to grace.

Having found what we've been looking for, we now have
the joy of giving it away. Forgiving people instead of judging
them. Seeing others as God sees them: in need of his love, in
need of his truth.

"Now my desire is to reach other Bad Girls...
women who can come to know Jesus
in a real relationship."

Think of the impact God can have through your life! If you surrender yourself to a vibrant relationship with Jesus, the women in your circle of influence may never be the same because of you. And because of grace.

After all, the gospel means "good news." And we have the best news in the world.

Let it shine, my friend!

Those who are wise
will shine
like the brightness of the heavens,
and those who lead many to righteousness,
like the stars
for ever and ever.

Daniel 12:3

BEFORE YOU TURN THE PAGE...

○ What elements of your past—whether sordid or solid—might God use to reach the hearts of other women?

○ If you grew up in a Christian home, how has that shaped you? And if you did not grow up in a Christian home, how has that shaped you?

○ Are your arms open wide, and your heart as well? If so, you're ready to help others embrace grace!

A Last Word from Liz

As you can tell from *Embrace Grace,* the women who read my books are dear to me and have taught me much. It blesses my soul to count you among them.

If you would enjoy receiving my free newsletter, *The Graceful Heart,* please visit my Web site—www.LizCurtisHiggs .com—or contact me by mail:

Liz Curtis Higgs
P.O. Box 43577
Louisville, KY 40253-0577

Until we meet again across the printed page, may God's grace abound in you!

Liz Curtis Higgs

P.S. Heartfelt thanks to a host of treasured editors and dear friends: Sara; Dudley; Jeanette; Laura; Carol; Glenna; hubby, Bill; cherished offspring, Matt and Lilly; and my two favorite Elizabeths, who read *Embrace Grace* in the early stages and offered godly wisdom and thoughtful advice. A special hug goes to a reader named Mary, who wrote, "Thanks for being willing to face the forgiven life." Blessings, one and all.

Continue your spiritual journey along with others
who've read these much-loved books by Liz Curtis Higgs:

Bad Girls of the Bible

"This book deeply touched me.
My eyes were misty as I read each page."

"I was convicted and challenged and found myself
digging through the Bible, rereading stories I thought I knew."

Really Bad Girls of the Bible

"Because of Liz's candor and vulnerability,
I exchanged the lies I had believed for the truth of God."

"As I read, I was reduced to tears of thanksgiving,
remorse, humility, awe, and love."

Unveiling Mary Magdalene

"This book took a figure robed in rumor and scandal
and turned her into a real person for me."

"I never thought a book would break me and speak to me the way
Unveiling Mary Magdalene did. I am truly a changed woman."

Rise and Shine: A Devotional

"When I started the first chapter, I just about cried.
It was like it was written for me."

"*Rise and Shine* has changed my life."

 WATERBROOK PRESS